You're in the Band SONGBOOK

Book 1

Audio tracks performed and recorded by Dave Clo

ISBN 978-1-4950-0232-8

WILLIS MUSIC

EXCLUSIVELY DISTRIBUTED BY

HAL•LEONARD®
CORPORATION

7777 W. BLUEMOUND RD. P.O. BOX 13819 MILWAUKEE, WI 53213

Visit Hal Leonard Online at
www.halleonard.com

HOW TO SAVE A LIFE

Words and Music by Joseph King and Isaac Slade

WHO'LL STOP THE RAIN

Words and Music by John Fogerty

CAN YOU FEEL THE LOVE TONIGHT

from Walt Disney Pictures' THE LION KING

Music by Elton John
Lyrics by Tim Rice

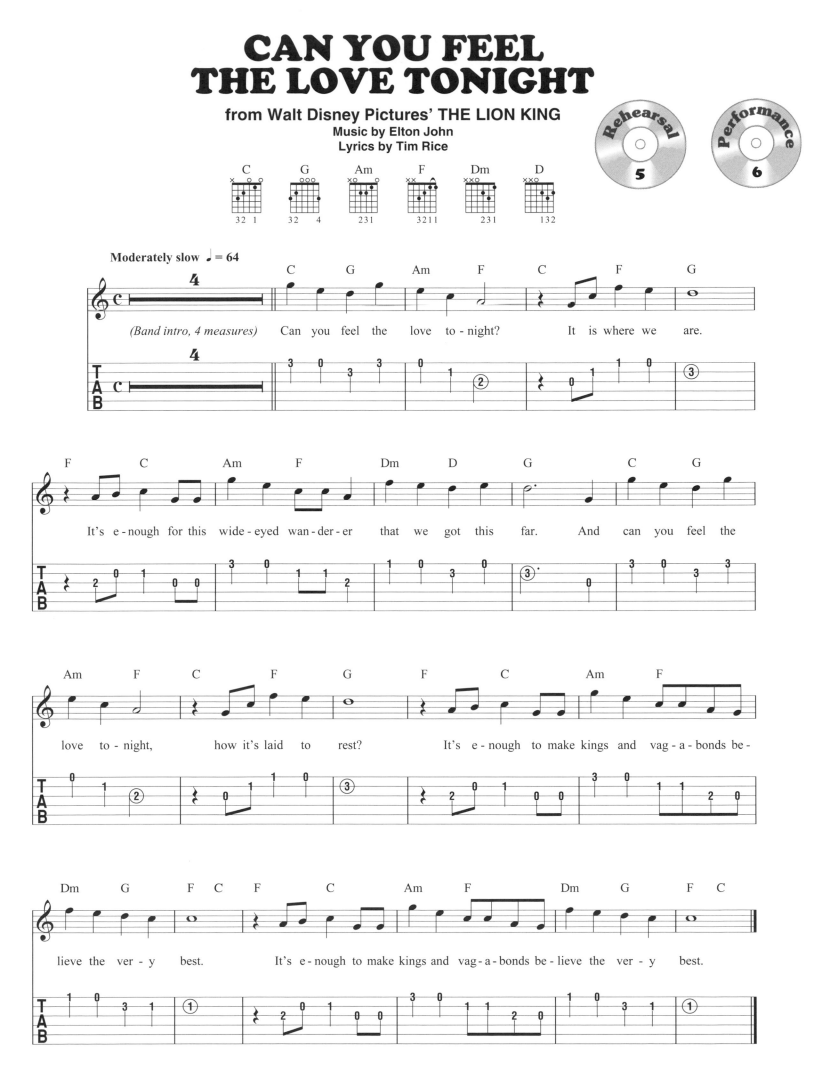

SHOUT

Words and Music by Roland Orzabal and Ian Stanley

black and white,   they real - ly, real - ly ought to know. ____

them good - bye.   You should - n't have to jump for joy. ____

Those   You should - n't have to... Shout, shout,

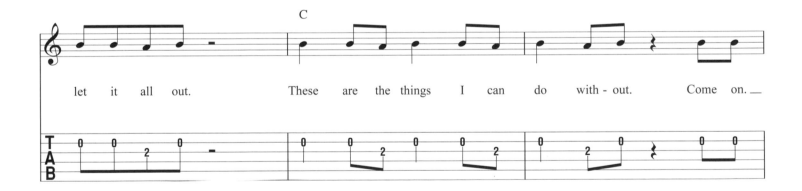

let it all out.   These are the things I can do with - out. Come on. __

__   I'm talk - ing to you. Come on. ____

ALL MY LOVING

Words and Music by John Lennon and Paul McCartney

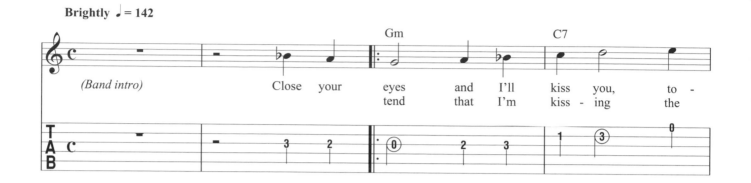

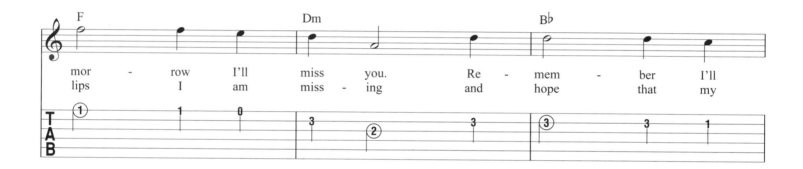

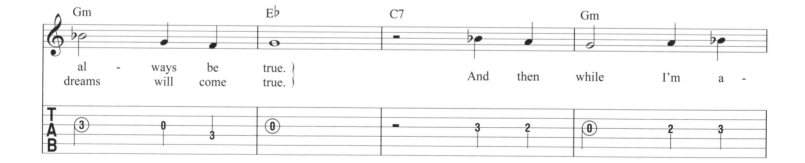

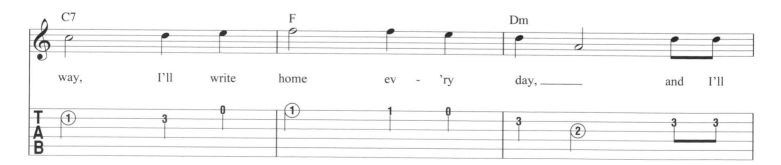

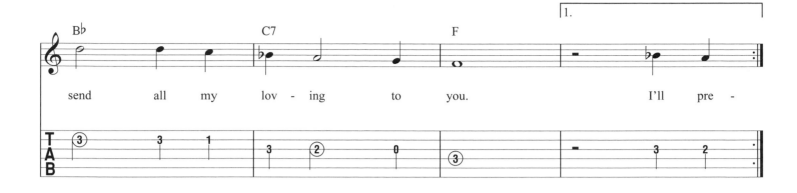

send   all   my   lov - ing   to   you.   I'll   pre -

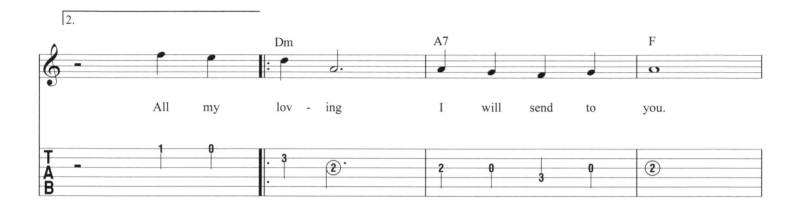

All   my   lov - ing   I   will   send   to   you.

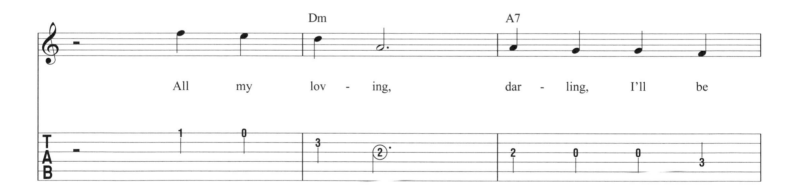

All   my   lov - ing,   dar - ling,   I'll   be

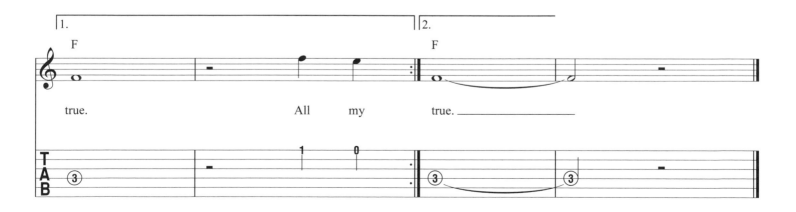

true.   All   my   true. _____

CLOCKS

Words and Music by Guy Berryman, Jon Buckland, Will Champion and Chris Martin

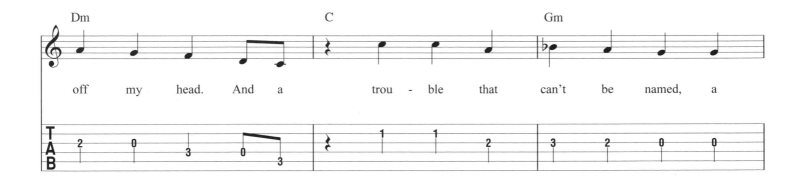

off my head. And a trou - ble that can't be named, a

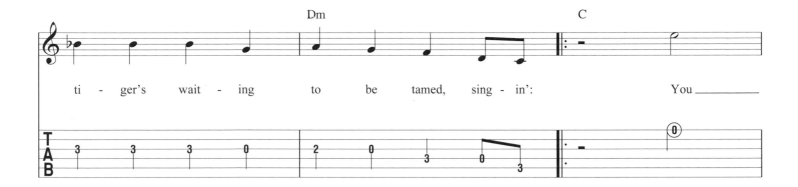

ti - ger's wait - ing to be tamed, sing - in': You _____

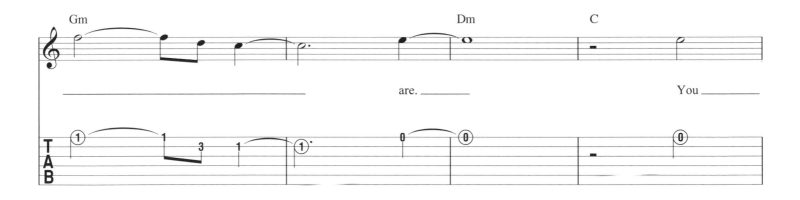

are. _____ You _____

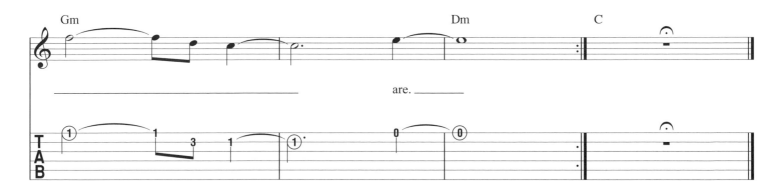

are. _____

I KNEW YOU WERE TROUBLE.

Words and Music by Taylor Swift, Shellback and Max Martin

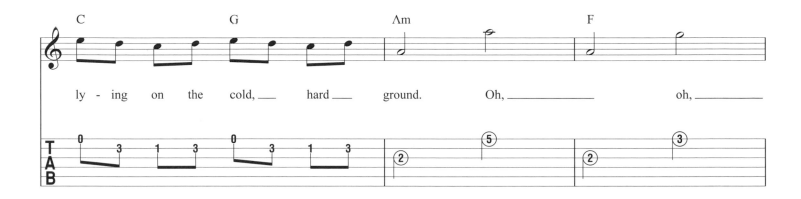

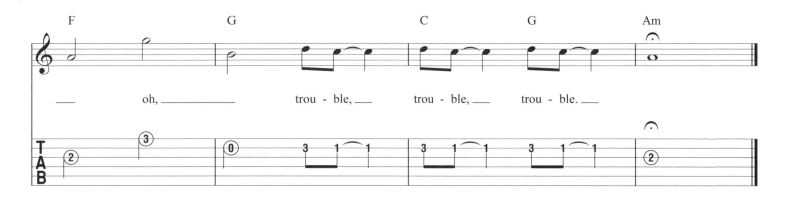

SWEET CAROLINE

Words and Music by Neil Diamond

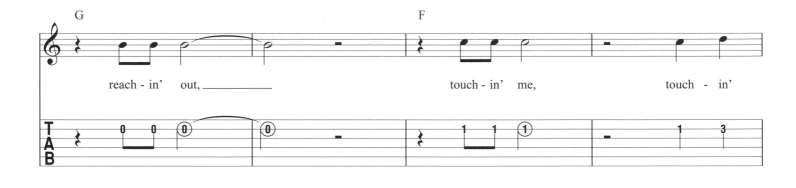

reach - in' out, _____ touch - in' me, touch - in'

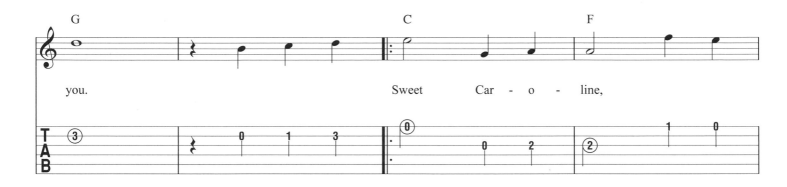

you. Sweet Car - o - line,

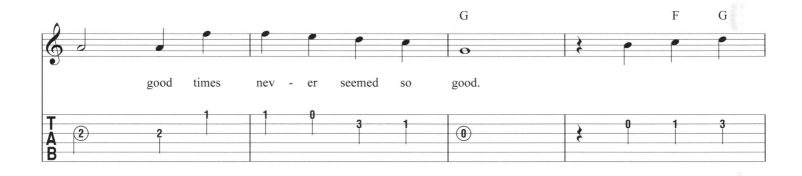

good times nev - er seemed so good.

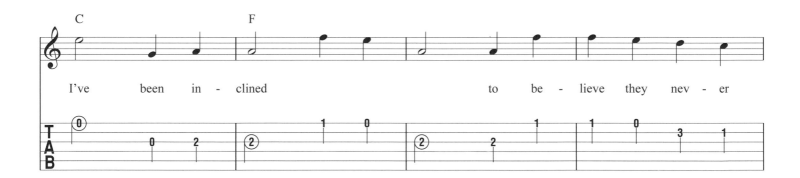

I've been in - clined to be - lieve they nev - er

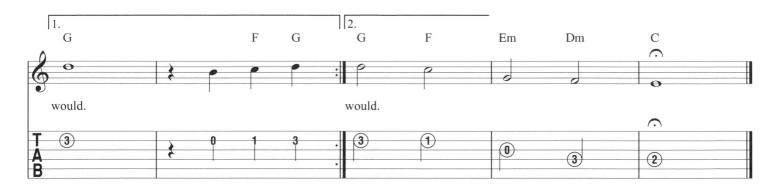

would. would.